1

DEMOCRATIZATION IN CUBA

A Concise Manual

JULIO M. SHILING

Translation by FRANK RODRÍGUEZ

Patria de Martí

Democratization in Cuba

Original title: *Democratización en Cuba*
Translated by Frank Rodríguez

Copyright © 2016 Julio M. Shiling
Copyright © 2016 Patria de Martí

Patria de Martí
Miami, Florida 33152
www.patriademarti.com
info@patriademarti.com

ISBN-13: 978-0692819708

First Spanish Edition: August 2016
First English Edition: December 2016

Printed in the United States of America

For Cuba that suffers and waits

Contents

Acknowledgements and gratitude

My debt of gratitude goes to José Tarano, technical producer and researcher for *Patria de Martí*, for his unwavering labor, whose work is indispensable in all our efforts to promote a culture of liberty, and to Frank Rodríguez who first edited this book in Spanish and later translated it into English, willing to work at all hours, in whose absence it would have been difficult to publish this work in a short time frame. To both of you, I extend my open hand in friendship!

My gratitude, above all else, to God y His heavenly order for making it all possible.

Towards a Democracy in Cuba

Since 1959, there exists in Cuba a totalitarian regime, of communist adherence with a sultanistic, patrimonial leadership type. It would be a grave mistake to believe that once the Castro-communist dictatorship falls, or announces a demolishing restructuring of itself, that Cuba invariably would become a democracy or be, by default, on its way to becoming a democracy. Democratization processes are full of pitfalls and mirages that try to thwart that feat. This work´s mission is to warn against these possibilities, unmask erroneous conceptualizations and to offer a proactive roadmap to successfully achieve and subsequently strengthen democracy in Cuba

A recommended course to follow could consist of a 10 Point Plan agenda, which appear listed and numbered in the following pages, and which espouses what needs to be carried out to assure a successful democratic transition and what should be part of a comprehensive state policy, of a free Cuban government. The forces that want to preserve the dictatorial status quo or its nuances and thus retain their privileges and be excused from any culpability for the ruin they caused in Cuba, will no doubt try to divert or limit the public discourse on change and liberalization, strictly within the economic realm. Therefore, all that is exposed and argued in this paper contains a strong resonance of urgency and importance. In no sense, however, does it seek to monopolize the discourse or discussion on this matter. The danger of sabotage to any democratization process, one must understand, is real. Castro-Communism has invested a great deal of time and capital trying to influence and manipulate public opinion, so that when the eminent moment of the debacle of the current dictatorial model heretofore is exercised, it be replaced with an adulterated version, one which is less antithetical than the existing model, but nonetheless far removed from the full establishment of Cuban democracy and the idea of a free and open society.

The two biggest challenges for a democratic transition are: (1) how to deal with the past; and (2) the consolidation of democratic institutions. The worst enemy of democratization is impunity. There is a clear connection of cause and effect between the challenges to reach democracy and its principal antagonist. If impunity is the variable that puts democracy at its greatest risk, then clearly it can be appreciated that treatment of the past, the need to assign responsibility to those who caused the horrific past to take place, the political mechanism that housed them, the consolidation of the Rule of Law and of democratic institutions such as an independent judiciary, all appear to point to the fact that a break in one impacts the rest, and that tolerance for criminal activity undermines the aspirations of being able to achieve and maintain a democratic model with full protection for civil and political liberties. All Ten Points focus on how to favorably deal, in a proactive fashion, with these two challenges in order to negate any possibility that impunity, the antithesis of the Rule of Law and a pivotal enemy of any democratization process, established a foothold in a new Cuba.

Liberation and Democratization

Democratization is not synonymous with liberation. They are two different processes and must be understood as such. The first that must occur is liberation. This means, in the case of Cuba, the collapse or cessation in command of power of the Castro regime. Liberation is part of a long struggle, a very costly and difficult one, which has been in progress for many years without a centralized command or a monolithic strategy or entity, but rather a historical process with the singular objective of achieving a Cuba, free of Communist despotism. The victory and honor of Cuban liberation will belong to those that resisted, supported and kept the faith that Cuba will, one day, be free. At that moment, and only parting from the time of liberation, once the Castro Communist control over political power concludes, is when the process of democratization can begin.

Democratization, understood rightfully as a process that begins with the demise of a dictatorial regime and seeks to establish and consolidate a democracy, constitutes a whole new struggle. It will be a different battle, where a new war will be waged against a series of dark and reactionary interests, which for different reasons, will try to sabotage Cuba's path to democracy. In the reconstruction of Cuba, to build the democratic edifice, it is imperative to differentiate between strategies that were applicable and relevant for the liberation process, but that are minutely connected with democratic formation, from a practical standpoint. Democracy-building, among other things, urges that priorities be placed on elevating social consciousness, as a basis of acquiring and successfully being able to apply democratic skills and ethics on a mass level.

The System is the Problem

In a democracy, transfers of power are an innate part of the system. There have been non-democratic regimes, definitely authoritarian in nature, which upon accepting to hold and respect free and competitive elections simply have accepted to abandon power, and this has been enough to guide the country into democracy, as was the case of General Pinochet who handed over power after a referendum he himself had called for. Totalitarian regimes, such as Communist or Fascists, do not offer this possibility to initiate a democratic transition with alternating administrations. In the matter of Castro-Communism, as the emblematic totalitarian dictatorship that it is, a wholesale dismantling is therefore called for. Why is this case?

The tyranny that has been dominating political power in Cuba since 1959 is not just a bad governmental entity. Castro-Communism is much more than a "government" in the strict sense of the word. A government is a political body in power to enact and enforce the laws of a State over a country or territory and its population. The dictatorship that operates in Communist Cuba is a *regime,* and this means that it includes within its model: its laws, its institutions, its ideology and socio-political system, its dominant party, its culture, its traditions and customs, its values and symbols, its leaders and its government. The responsibility for the inhumanity in Cuba falls upon the regime and the system that sustained it ideologically.

If on the one hand the leadership of the Castro regime has been dominated by the Castro brothers, under no concept does responsibility go to this family alone. It is true that "Castro-Communism" follows the reality of how it came to be: a regime of total domination, ideologically subservient and identified as Communist, founded out of a molded leadership structure of extreme personalism, known in the social sciences as *Sultanistic.* In other words, even though the Castro tyrants undoubtedly have headed the top of the culprits, however, international Communism has been the systemic gene and the ideological spine that has supported this perversity exerted from power. The Communist system, its party, the ideology and the tyrannical Cuban regime, together with the top echelon that includes the Castro's and their accomplices, they all share responsibility.

What is democracy?

Democracy is a socio-political system of self-government, where sovereignty resides with the people who enter into a social contract with a group of people in order to constitute a government, elected by them and responsible to them, to govern them, while they, the sovereign people, retain the option to remove their confidence in it so as to select others in periodic, free and competitive elections, in an environment that guarantees respect for fundamental freedoms, and such a social contract is to be reinforced by the Rule of Law. Democracy is not an economic system. Despots love to incorporate economic and material factors to try to merge them into the understanding of what constitutes a democracy. This demagogical practice is relied upon by totalitarian tyrants, especially in search of legitimacy or to hide gross violations of inalienable rights and values.

Limits of power, the separation into branches of government and the autonomy of these institutions, are intrinsic aspects of democracy. Checks and balances to the system keep the necessary equilibrium for a pluralistic society to be free and to live in social harmony.

In a democracy the Rule of Law is in force, that is, the *Law has supremacy* which is not the same as a "legal government". Under the Rule of Law the existence of preeminent rights totally outside the purview of any government are acknowledged. In other words, no government, without any conventional law or constitutional article can transgress natural rights. These come from God. One is born with them and no democratic government can overtake that barrier found in Natural Law. On the other hand, a legal government can issue unjust laws that violate elemental precepts in order to punish those that break the law. This absence of limits or checks regarding what is preeminent is the difference in the two understandings of an ethical and legal principle. To provide an example, the horror that allowed the Holocaust in Nazi Germany was harbored by Fascists laws.

<u>The Main Purpose of a Democratic Government</u>

The most important task of a government that answers to a democratic regime is to protect those natural rights in a society, fundamental among them is liberty. That is what ethically holds primacy. Providing goods and services to the citizenry plays a role for sure, a valuable role in the responsibilities of a government, but it is not its main obligation, rather a secondary one. However, dictatorships feed off of the distortion of elemental principles that make up a democracy and of the fundamentals contained in the doctrine of self-government and its primary relationship with the defense of basic freedoms.

The Danger of Prioritizing the Economy

When the Communist assaulted power in Russia in 1917 launching their global war against the democratic order, the schematic doctrine of a Socialist economy that they employed, based on perceived laws of History and economic determinism, was one of centralized planning of the state's means of production, using five-year plans and fundamental collectivism. This represented opposite poles between the Communist orbit and the free world which was following its unique model, capitalism, with free markets and the means of production in private hands. The quantitative difference between the two regimes and its respective systems of values and ethics was easy to discern. The reformulation of the Socialist model incorporating capitalist notions, recognizing market fundamentals, tolerating private property and actively performing as actors in globalization, has caused disturbances in the political and ethical environments.

Business interests, the amorality of the markets and a world increasingly intertwined by economic links, has been a disservice to democracy. False equivalencies have been established which serve only to legitimize dictatorial regimes. It is true that capitalism has shown its superiority regarding the production of goods and services in a more effective way, both qualitatively as quantitatively, however, it has also proven its inability to transfer its complementary political model by nature of democracy, exemplified by the case of totalitarian dictatorships such as that of the Chinese Communist Party.

The Danger of Stagnating in Despotism

The adoption of market mechanisms and the acceptance of privatizing the means of production (up to a point), although these continue to remain dominated by the dictatorial political power, have produced newfangled variants of Socialism. Asian Communism, essentially a hybrid model that combines a Leninist State with a mixed economy, has shown proof of being able to produce a prototype of governance that has been immune to democratic contagion or to be able to overcome perennial misery while it continues to survive as a tyrannical system.

The globalized economy and the acclimatization of perverted and adulterated versions of capitalism have incapacitated a great deal of the world's political class preventing it from acting in solidarity to resist and try to revert these new formulations of dictatorships, not only the ones such as Asian Communism but also those of Putin in Russia and of Socialism of the 21st Century in Latin America. The liberalization of the exclusive realm of the economy is a recipe for despotisms' survival.

The Danger of the Return of Despotism

Democratic transitions have shown little uniformity in achieving a successful ending. Some have, others have never taken off and some others have reverted, such that after establishing democracy they have fallen, returning to a dictatorial regime. These things don't happen out of the blue. Today there is enough empirical evidence to be able to determine, beforehand, those factors that contributed to those results.

Totalitarian dictatorships, as is the case of Castro-Communism, require the complete dismantling of the regime. That alone is not sufficient. A host of legal, ethical and political measures are needed to ensure that the system has been wholesale erased. Additionally, it is vital to nail down legislation, to incorporate mechanisms and to adopt sensible policies to disincentives inconformity and to block its reappearance, perhaps dressed up in different costumes, of the same evil that has beaten down Cuba for so many years.

What follows are the ten points that try to encompass the main factors needed to reach and to institutionalize democracy in Cuba.

Point 1 Transitional Justice

As the name implies, *transitional justice* is designed to serve as a transitory mechanism to enable a transformation from a dictatorship to a democracy. In the specific cases where the starting point is a totalitarian regime, as is the case in Castro Communism, its implementation is indispensable. Outside an ethical and legal framework of this kind, Cuba would run into great difficulties in its project to achieve democratization. Absent a process of transitional justice the possibilities open to Cuban democrats would be seriously impaired. All modifications or changes that could be suggested would not be able to gain steam toward the goal of Cuba becoming a democracy. Rather we would see the permanence of a non-democratic state of affairs.

What is transitional justice? It is the accumulation of legal, ethical and political measures that seeks to alleviate the damages occasioned to a society that has suffered systematic violations of human rights. Transitional justice facilitates the road to the establishment of democratic institutions. Without the institutionalism of a democratic regime, the Rule of Law cannot appear. That is why this process serves as a bridge for any nation that seeks transformation from a dictatorial regime to a democratic one. It is an indispensable democratizing and purifying tool!

This is a convincing and incontrovertible point. Absent the aforementioned legal process, to reiterate, Cuba would probably drift into another dictatorial species of the Chinese/Vietnamese variant (Asian Communism), oligarchic despotism akin to Putin's Russia, another 21st century dictatorship, or into a failed State. The reason is simple. Transitional justice focuses directly on the first fundamental challenge to the process of democratization: dealing with the past. Any attempt to dodge this, to annul the *collective memory* of a people, would hold disastrous results for a democratic transition. This would frustrate the wished-for genuine *reconciliation.* It would only prolong the inevitable time for the Cuban nation to reconcile a traumatic past with the systematic violation of all *natural rights* for which there are no statutes of limitation as they are preeminent, with the repairing notion that the evil exerted from the political power can be repaired by means of an orderly, equitable and fair process.

From the starting point that all roads to democratization require dealing with the past, transitional justice focuses directly on this first existential challenge. Specifically, this set of legal/ethical/political measures seeks to fulfill three essential things: (1) to shed light on crimes (2) punish the guilty; (3) to indemnify the victims. This serves multiple important purposes in an incipient democracy, as would be the case of the Cuban democracy after the long stay of totalitarianism.

For this task a free and democratic Cuban State should lend a hand with all mechanisms at its disposal. The Ministry of Justice should be the governmental institution charged with bringing up charges and proceeding with the role of prosecutor, in cooperation with other law enforcement agencies. The documentation and research to ease this legal process can be assisted by information from private institutions, individuals or foreign States that wish to cooperate. However, it will be up exclusively to the free Cuban State to determine the merits of such information or testimony as well as the decision to present charges or not against any accused. Investigations and judgments in the process of transitional justice will guarantee to anyone accused the *due process of law.*

Regarding secrets files held by the Castro Communist regime that may contain documentation about any criminal, subversive or illegal activity need to be made public. This includes all the operations of control and repression, espionage, blackmail, arrests, murders, deportations, tortures, mob actions, clinical experiments, extortions, exploitations and any manner of denigrating actions against the human condition, either directed or tolerated by the Castro dictatorship. This information and its disposition to the public, to prosecutors, to private detectives, to scholars and to the international community has the expressed purpose of serving as a database for researchers that may be useful in clearing up crimes whose evidence could be used in future trials.

The free and democratic Cuban State needs to display all this enormous amount of information about the crimes committed and the subversive and illicit activities of the Castro dictatorship that have taken place inside and outside of Cuba against both Cuban and foreign nationals. These files should be digitized and made permanently available, in addition to being preserved in a physical site. Although this function could make use of data and cooperation from human rights States (OAS), the United Nations (UN), the International Court of Justice, etc., it needs to remain under the jurisdiction of a Cuban governmental agency whose partial responsibility would be to search, organize, store, digitize, preserve and facilitate its access to the Cuban society and to the world. A new ministry perhaps named: Ministry of Memory and Defense of Liberty and Democracy (more about this ministry under Principle Number 3) could be established.

The three objectives mentioned for transitional justice look to empower Cuban society, making clear what are some of the rights that victims of violations committed by institutions have against the dictatorship. Cuban society has the right to know the truth and to have a collective memory. The systematic violations of human rights and crimes against humanity have to be clarified. This procedure would additionally cement the rights of Cubans to see justice prevail by punishment of the culprit or culpable. Transitional justice guarantees, with the third right, that victims receive just reparations for these crimes.

To summarize this fundamental point, when in a country a government and its institutions have committed gross violations of human rights and State crimes, society has the right to a concrete *elucidation* of the crime, to *punish* the guilty and to *indemnify* the victims. These are crucial steps in the construction of a democratic regime. Why is this so important? After all, some argue that it is best to forget, proposing a sort of *fresh start*. Wouldn't that be better for democratization?

Transitional justice should not be confused with *truth commissions*. At first glance, it would seem that both achieve the same purpose. However, this is not the case. Truth commissions focus their work on the first task of transitional justice: to elucidate the crime. They are not able to execute the other two functions: to punish the guilty; and to indemnify the victims. In totalitarian dictatorships such as Castro's, a truth commission would be a great disservice to the process of democratization, as it would in practice promote *impunity*. It would not reconcile a free and democratic present with its tormented and dictatorial past, as it would exclude the relief sought by the victim and the sanction for those responsible. That is

why we emphasize that a truth commission is not a substitute for transitional justice.

All non-democratic regimes commit crimes and violate human rights. All nations that have suffered dictatorships have the right to the fulfillment of the three goals of transitional justice (elucidate crimes, punish the culprits, indemnify the victims). However, for regimes of total domination, such as the type of despotism exhibited in Cuba since 1959, transitional justice is a mandatory prescription. Communist and Fascist dictatorships are both totalitarian, as we have reiterated. One of the characteristics of these political models is their adhesion to a *radical ideology.*

Ideologies of a radical bent, in contrast to democratic ideologies, are in effect *political religions.* It doesn't matter if the ideology is taken from a belief system or from political rhetoric. Totalitarian regimes rationalize their conduct from the starting point of their understanding and optic of the world. Viewed from that prism, they trample on the worth of the individual and on the basic liberties that stand in the way of their ideological objectives. For Communists, the world supposedly obeys laws of History that manifest in class warfare. Fascists rest their vision in the perception of laws of Nature that express themselves in race wars or wars among nations. They are first cousins who have held on to ideologies that have caused many deaths and other crimes against humanity "justified" by those sets of ideas that accompany their *political action* plans.

The fraudulent mystique that an ideology such as Communism establishes necessitates a *moral judgment* on the practical and theoretical model. Transitional justice does precisely this. The systematic violation of natural and human rights impacts not only those that have suffered it directly but the trauma also extends indirectly on the collective psyche of a society. Dismantling generalized propaganda, falsified history and invented myths is required, all that has been engendered to propitiate a *counterculture.* The social defenestration that any totalitarian society suffers while the dictatorial model reigns requires that barbarism be criminalized and not glorified.

Democracy, a socio-political self-government model, with its approach of absolute respect for preeminent (natural) rights, the separation of powers within the government and the prioritization of tolerance and pluralism, requires for its proper functioning the *Rule of Law.* This is much more than the government following the guidelines of "laws". Dictatorships gain legitimacy and commit crimes against humanity applying unjust "laws". There is a big difference between a *legal government* and the *Rule of Law.* The former is the mere obedience of written laws. These, however, may be unfair. In Nazi Germany and Communist China, for example, inhumanity was enforced (still going on in China) following the letter of the "law". The Rule of Law, however, recognizes the existence of preeminent (natural rights) rights outside the realm of any *conventional law.* In other words, there are rights that no government can take away because they come from God, and precede the existence of any government or *social contract.*

For the Rule of Law to hold sway, an independent judicial branch has to enforce respect for the law. This is achieved following all conventional laws but also always prioritizing the parameters of natural rights. In order to achieve all this, the antithesis of the Rule of Law, *impunity,* cannot be tolerated. Transitional justice is helpful in combating this visceral enemy to democratization. All democracies, particularly nascent ones, have the right to zero tolerance for impunity. If not, it is akin to extending an open invitation for despotism to return with a red carpet reception.

Transitional justice is that, the cornerstone on that foundation upon which democracy is built. To provide for a genuine and whole national reconciliation that would turn into a free, open and democratic society, this legal/ethical/political process is indispensable. The most successful cases of democratization in totalitarian tyrannies such as from Nazism towards democracy have all placed transitional justice as a priority in the democratization program. In Cuba it is of equal importance and will have the same favorable results that have been achieved in other democracies where it has been implemented.

Additionally, all current prison sentences in Cuban jails should be reviewed, to assure that the politicized dictatorial judicial system did not hand out false and unwarranted sentences. All political prisoners, of course, would have been freed immediately upon the initial moment of liberation.

Point 2 Decommunization

Decommunization is another legal/ethical/political process which, in this case, seeks to completely eradicate the tyrannical *modus operandi* of Castro Communism. Its specific purpose is the obliteration of the Castro regime, both in the abstract as in practice. Decommunization contains, as part of its propitiating project, another procedure known as *lustration*. In practice by a government in the process of democratic gestation, lustration is, typically, a set of laws designed to avoid having officials of the previous dictatorship and others responsible for crimes associated with the dictatorial domination participation in public life, particularly in politics.

Decommunization, in its entirety, is an indispensable course to be taken to initiate the reversion of the anthropological, psychological and historical damage that Cuban Communism has been inflicting upon Cuba since 1959. With the measures taken under this project the goal will be to prevent Castro Communism's return to power ever again. This process of decontamination will also facilitate the establishment and subsequent strengthening of democratic institutions and of civil society. Taking into account the implications of a legal nature, a branch of the Ministry of Justice needs to be charged with reinforcing this program.

The Cuban Communist Party (CCP) is the instrumental agent from which all the tentacles of the dictatorship emanate. As such, it is the first organism that will directly fall under decommunization. The CCP needs to be shut down as an operating entity, together with all its appendices. This encompasses, naturally, the political police, community organizations, intelligence bodies, the upper echelon of the armed forces, the government structure (all its branches), paramilitary corps and the management of government-run companies. When we talk of the CCP, we naturally include adaptations or particular interpretations of "Fidelism", "Raulism" or any other similar variation thereof. Castro Communism, as a tyrannical phenomena and political mass was the one that selected, formed and utilized the CCP as its motorized facade, and therefore it is the most relevant and precise institution where to begin the process of systematically dismembering and dismantling it in Cuba.

In totalitarian dictatorships, this monolithic party absorbs the State once it consolidates in power. This is another objective of decommunization: to free the State from its dictatorial Party, separating them. No democratic State can be the personification of a movement or of a particular party. Communism and Fascism have appropriated the State each time they have reached power, and from there have operated as criminal organizations under the legitimizing clothing of the State. The particularities of Castro's despotism, as we have argued, turn it into a *sui generis* case, as this model combines a series of atypical characteristics within the dictatorial Socialist camp. The Castro dictatorship, in addition to being a totalitarian regime of the Communist ideological type, this variant has exercised, throughout its history, a type of leadership that can be categorized as *charismatic sultanistic*. This means that within an absolutist governmental scheme with a high dosage of personalistic and arbitrary leadership, it adopts, additionally, dynastic and nepotistic overtones.

In addition to the dissolution of the CCP and its institutions, it would also be necessary to ensure its prohibition as a political organization that can compete in democratic elections. Outlawing the CCP is necessary mainly for three reasons. Specifically, in the

Cuban case this organization was the culprit of record of all the crimes committed by the Castro Communist regime because the Party/State was merged by the upper echelon of the dictatorial ruler removing any vestige that the CCP may have had of being a "political party" in the civilized and democratic sense of the word. The CCP is a criminal enterprise, conceived with the expressed and deliberate purpose of validating and carrying out the assignments of a tyrannical regime. It is not now and never was a political party in the technical and functional sense of the word or in its application within the context of a comparative democratic context. This has been another false equivalency that the radical left has insisted on promoting.

The proscription of the CCP makes it impossible for an *anti-system* political entity to be able to have the opportunity to subvert the democratic order, arriving to power through democratic means to then, once in control, break down its institutions to reinsert despotism. Hitler's and Mussolini's victories at the ballot box make this abundantly clear, the danger that democracies run when they provide space for anti-system movements to compete for political power. Whoever doesn't play by democratic rules need not be allowed to participate in the democratic game! European democracies, after their liberation from Fascist despotism in 1945, formulated laws prohibiting the participation in the democratic political process of political parties from that persuasion. These laws are still in force today in almost all of Europe.

The action of vetoing the CCP from the political process in a free and democratic Cuba doesn't mean that people with ideological affinity for Communist, Fascists, anarchist, fundamental Islam or other radical ideologies will not be able to exercise their rights to freely express themselves, to associate, to publish or to spread their ideas publicly. Even in the case of persons with an attraction towards Marxist perspectives, there is space in the wide political spectrum within the democratic left to welcome them; social democrats are another example of this. The important thing behind this measure is not to annul the right of people to think or express themselves. The *pluralism* we long for in Cuba points to Cubans having diverse political and ideological options. However, democracy, as a political model of popular self-government, within the framework of the Rule of Law, imposes limits. The limitations are to be applied to safeguard democracy and to ensure that Cubans may be able to remain in an open and free society. The limits, it must be emphasized, are imposed more directly on the government, whose main role is to defend the liberty of its citizens, to reinforce the Rule of Law and, consequently, to safeguard the democratic model from toxic and lethally damaging movements against its existence.

In addition to the disarticulation and invalidation of the CCP, what would be other specific tasks of decommunization in Cuba? The answer is that there are many things to do and all are necessary. The idea is not to validate the tyrannical domination that Cuba has suffered since 1959, nor to tolerate its apologists, or to promote the impunity or to facilitate its return to power, it is crucial to spread out the process to all national strata where the Castro regime has spread. Only then can totalitarianism and its sequels be reverted.

One of the main purposes of decommunization is to ensure that all the members of the CPP in positions of public authority in the political, social, economic, military, cultural, legal and educational environments of the country are removed from their posts. This action seeks to deny access to people who performed a role of functional and relevant complicity in the maintenance of the Castro Communist system to the nerve centers of a society that is looking to secure its democratic institutions. Those people would not be impeded from working in the private sector or to be self-employed.

All the symbolism, insignias and paraphernalia utilized or associated with the Cuban Communist regime needs to be removed from all public spaces, as well as the permanent banishment of displaying them again in public. This includes the elimination of all statues, monuments or other structures that pay homage to people, institutions, movements, parties, alliances, etc., tied or that have served the interest of Castro Communism. This effort also covers the annulment of the observation of holidays, occasions and celebrations linked to the Cuban dictatorship. The names of streets, towns, parks, institutes, buildings, industries and the dictatorial historiography, etc., that came from the Castro regime would need to be changed. It is not advisable to tolerate the apology for the inhuman barbarism of the regime. In Europe, after World War II ("WWII"), again, the democracies of the continent established clear laws with the goal of guarding against apologists. Cubans, applying the same common sense, should draw up laws tending to prohibit any apology for the Castro dictatorship.

In contrast to transitional justice, which proposes the task of taking care of specific cases of violations of human rights and crimes against humanity empowering the victims (investigate the crime, indemnify the victim) and assigning responsibility to the criminals (punishing the guilty), decommunization centers on the removal from public life and the public arena all of the Castro regimes symbolism, its institutions, laws, the comprehensive power structure (political, military, educational, cultural, legal and economic), and the derived privileges of all its leaders and influential players.

Some may think that in a dictatorship of total domination as the Castro Communist one, it would be difficult to find people who have not in some way, at some time, been part of the State machinery. This is not true. Undoubtedly, one of the greatest perversions of Communist and Fascist regimes is that their public dominion extends to every nook and cranny of the life of the individual. However, typically, only a very small portion of the society is directly responsible for the crimes of the State, of crimes against humanity, of gross violations of human rights and other criminal acts such as corruption, theft, abuse of power, etc., that were committed. The empirical evidence shows this.

The successful exit of totalitarianism towards democracy has seen in all cases some variation of the process of decommunization or denazification (equivalent to decommunization but applicable to German Fascism.) Additionally, it has been precisely that in countries where there was little or no process of this kind where democracy never took hold or where the existing socio-political model simply remained as a variation of despotism. The most successful democratic transitions from totalitarianism to democracy, to reiterate, have exhibited these processes without exception. Since the fall of Soviet Communism several countries from the former Socialist bloc began the process of decommunization starting in the 1990s. In all the cases (if ever) a very miniscule portion of the society was sanctioned. In the most emblematic legal case of anti-totalitarian decontamination of all the dictatorships of total domination, the case of Nazi Germany after the conclusion of WWII sheds light on an example that allows us to illustrate this point.

In 1946, upon the fall of Fascist despotism in Europe, Germany's population was a bit over 65 million people. Denazification forced nearly 6 million Germans to face legal proceedings (less than 10% of the population). Of these, however, only 20% received any kind of penalty and almost none went to jail or were executed. To be more accurate, the numbers of those that faced the most severe sentences or capital punishment were 1,600 people (the cases of the application of capital punishment were very small). This is the equivalent of less than 0.00003076923 of the total population, very much less than even 1% of the population! If we were to apply this sequence of numbers in proportion to the population of Cuba today we would be talking about less than 350 people. These numbers, of course, are hypothetical and only for the purposes of comparison and to establish the seminal point that only a very small amount of people would in practice face the weight of the process of decontamination of totalitarianism.

Decommunization, we can conclude, offers numerous services to a democratic transition. The most valuable is the moral judgment that is made of it and the overwhelming verdict that falls upon a Communist dictatorship that has governed tyrannically for more than 57 years, with the selective arbitrariness of privileging its cronies and family members while distressing an entire people, denying them their natural rights and forcing them into exile in order to be free.

Point 3 Publish International Subversion and Crimes

Castro Communism has not only damaged Cubans. His dictatorial span has reached outside Cuba as his terrorist and hegemonic activity has extended throughout the globe. Consequently, the victims of Castro's dictatorship are found in all continents holding a multitude of passports. The free and democratic Cuban State would have a moral obligation to democratic ethics, committing to making public all available information regarding subversive, criminal and illicit activities. The objective would be to assist in any foreign investigation to shed light on crimes or to offer evidence that may be used to condemn the criminals.

The democratic Cuban government, however, would not be in the financial shape to indemnify non-Cubans as part of the process of Cuban transitional justice, but it would offer all manner of cooperation in the extradition of any individual implicated in a crime facilitating to legal authorities abroad all the support material at the disposal of Cuban authorities. A universal sense of values and all fundamental rights have no expiration date, and international democratic solidarity carries the moral imperative for the new democratic Cuban nation to work on the deserving task of instituting and preserving all files so that any person or institution from any part of the world might be able to access them electronically or in person, all of it free of charge. The information regarding international subversion and crime would be housed in the archives of the Ministry of Memory and Defense of Liberty and Democracy.

It is important to remember that Communist Cuba served the interests of international Communism grandiloquently; fighting against the democratic order in the world from the time Castro came to political power, not only in a consistent manner but with seminal implications. From January 1, 1959, Castro Communism intended on becoming a primordial change agent of Marxist-Leninism in the American continent and to be a close ally of this same purpose in the rest of the world. The thousands of deaths and other gross damages that Cuban Communism has brought about in the global scene, directly or indirectly, are irrefutable. Its subversive and terrorist interference in the affairs of other countries, its intentions, consisting in bringing down the democratic order, have been a chronic course of action which has impacted many nations. As well his extraterritorial activism in illicit efforts have included complicity in kidnappings, the practice of torture, killings and murders, participation in and facilitation of drug trafficking, money laundering, influence peddling, bribery, etc.

This magnanimous role in international subversion, which the Castro regime attributed unto itself and carried out, was able to be accomplished with the massive operation of tens of thousands of individuals, financed by practically unlimited resources outside the public scrutiny of any source included: the coffers of the former Union of Soviet Socialist Republics, Venezuela, radical Islam (notably Iran), finance from banks and credit agencies in democratic countries, profits from hidden enterprises, drug traffic, confiscations of properties and assets, sale of intelligence information about the U.S., leasing Cuban territory for Chinese and Russian espionage against the U.S., and the newfangled practice of slavery represented by the leasing of Cuban professionals in the Third World or to international organisms.

Terrorism, as a methodology to attain political power, became manifest in the actions of the rural and urban guerrillas which Castro organized, guided, trained, financed, backed and served as apologist throughout Latin America from the time he took over Cuba. Castro's Communism formed a series of institutions to execute its subversive plans. They are made up by organisms directly connected to the dictatorial Castro State, front institutions that pretend to be NGOs or community organizations, as well as continental and international organs created explicitly for this purpose.

Among the main government institutions directly linked at the departmental or quasi-departmental level of the Cuban Communist dictatorship and with responsibilities over international subversive operations are or have been: the General Intelligence Directorate, the America Department, the Military Intelligence Directorate and the Counter-Intelligence Directorate. Each of these institutions has had at times subdivisions under their command. The Ministry of Foreign Relations cannot be excluded. This ministry, one of the most used by Communist Cubans for conspiratorial interference, is in fact a diplomatic shield that provides the cover of a facade for a great deal of espionage and counter-espionage.

Institutions such as the Organization for Solidarity with the Peoples of Africa, Asia and Latin America, the Organization of Latin American Solidarity (both products of the Havana Tricontinental Conference), the Movement of Non-Aligned Countries, the Forum of São Paulo, the ALBA, Bolivarian Alliance for the Peoples of Our America and the CELAC, Community of Latin American and Caribbean States, are some of the inter-governmental mechanisms that the Castro's have engendered or where they have exerted a dominant influence in order to advance the interests of international Communism, also known as real Socialism and its readapted offspring, Socialism of the 21st Century.

Front organizations that have been or continue to be extensions of the dictatorial power or instrumental in subversive goals include: the Institute for Friendship with the Peoples, Casa de las Americas, and Prensa Latina (press agency). All the aforementioned organizations do not cover the totality of the subversive machinery and are only a sample of the more relevant organisms of international subversion. Next we will mention some of the movements with which Castro Communism has cooperated throughout the years.

We include here some of the terrorist organizations that received aid from the Castro criminal project in promoting its imperialist agenda: Popular Movement for the Liberation of Angola; Liberation Armed Forces, Revolutionary Army of the People, Guerrilla Army of the People, Montoneros (Argentina); Bolivarian Communist Party, National Liberation Army (Che Guevara's guerrilla invasion), Movement Towards Socialism (Bolivia); Worker's Party (Brazil); Movement of the Revolutionary Left, Patriotic Front Manuel Rodríguez (Chile); Revolutionary Armed Forces of Colombia, National Liberation Army, April 19 Movement, Medellin Cartel (Colombia); Rebels of Simba (another of Guevara's adventures in Congo); PAIS Alliance(Ecuador); Farabundo Martí Front for National Liberation (El Salvador); ETA (Spain); Communist Party USA, Black Panthers, Weather Underground (U.S.); Moros Front (Philippines); Guerrilla Army of the People, National Guatemalan Revolutionary Union (Guatemala); Party for the Independence of Guinea and Cabo Verde; IRA (Northern Ireland); Red Brigades (Italy); New Jewel Movement

(Jamaica); Japanese Red Army (Japan); Mozambique Liberation Front; Sandinista National Liberation Front (Nicaragua); Popular Front for the Liberation of Palestine, Organization for the Liberation of Palestine, Hamas, Islamic Resistance Movement, Black September (Palestine); Movement of the Revolutionary Left,
Túpac Amaru Resistence Movement; Shining Path (Peru); Macheteros, National Liberation Armed Forces (Puerto Rico); Hezbohla (Iran-Lebanon); Dominican Patriotic Union (Dominican Republic); National African Congress (South Africa); National Liberation Movement, Oriental Revolutionary Movement, Tupamaros (Uruguay); Movement of the Revolutionary Left, Revolutionary Communist Party, National Liberation Armed Forces, Bolivarian Revolutionary Movement 200, Fifth Republic Movement (Venezuela).

We have provided a partial list of movements with the name of the countries to posit that the terrorist behavior of the Castro dictatorship spread throughout the world, and all that this sinister facilitation has cost; this needs to be made known.

Point 4 Identify and Recuperate Secret and Ill-gotten Assets, and Illicit Enrichment

Our evidence shows, irrefutably, that Castro Communism has embezzled billions of dollars for the personal gain of the governing elite. Additionally, it has forged a very wide network of for-profit enterprises, some identifiable, some secret, and without any form of public scrutiny. This capital and other corporate structures belong to the Cuban nation and not to a dictatorial oligarchy. A Cuban free and democratic State has the responsibility of investigating and expediting the due process of law against these individuals and their family members and companies that took part in this national plunder in order to recover these assets. All that is able to be recuperated should go into a special fund to be used exclusively to indemnify first the victims of the crimes committed by this regime and later to cover expenses related to the reconstruction of Cuba. A Commission for the Recovery of Ill-gotten Funds should be established.

It is estimated that, according to sources from the rank and file of the Castro power base, more than 100 Cubans are millionaires. The list could be longer and here we are talking about, only those figures that appear in the governing highest echelon. Fidel Castro, the one who stole the most, a net worth of a billion dollars was estimated at the time of his death. In all of these cases these fortunes were obtained illicitly, as gangsters are prone to do, and at the expense of the Cuban people. The methodology employed for this illicit enrichment has followed different paths in order to prey on the nation.

In addition to the widespread and systematic corruption existing in Communist Cuba, spread throughout all social strata, the largest stolen capital is distributed from the highest spheres of the power structure. In other words, the distribution of all that is looted operates with the authorization of the Castro brothers or their closest aides. Cuban Communism in the exercise of political domination has operated, invariably, as an organized crime family (a Mafia).

The extracting of a percentage of the profits of State enterprises, inside and outside Cuba, represents one of the more common ways of outrageous enrichment prevalent in Cuba. Everything relating to tourism means that

100% of the foreign exchange that enters Cuba makes a stop first in the personal coffers of these people. The remittances sent by the Cuban Diaspora, historically, have always been detoured in part into the pockets of the Castro bourgeoisie. The dictatorship also preys on the personal worth of the dominant caste taking another percentage off of what they pillage from Cuban workers sent to work abroad, whose labor is leased out. In anything having to do with electronics: cell phones, computers, tablets, etc., which require a continual payment of money for their use; a portion is destined to go to the gangsters at the top of the food chain. The illegal enrichment, however, has not been limited to the appropriation of a slice of something of value that enters Cuba or lands in the hands of Cubans.

The new rich who attained millionaire status by the hand of the political power dictatorship have also enriched themselves selling off properties confiscated unlawfully. Works of art, jewels, luxury items, antiques, real estate, etc., are some of the properties that have been trafficked for the personal enrichment of a few. The Cuban Communist dictatorship has spared no effort in connecting with the best auctioneers in the world to bring to market tangible assets expropriated in the name of the revolution and under the Marxist-Leninist slogan, while the profits coming from these sales, however, went into the coffers of the tyrant Fidel Castro, and to those he grants permission to partake in these activities.

Castro Communism has turned, since its arrival in power, to activities that are totally outside the parameters of what is moral or ethical. The drug traffic has been another business which has provided high profit margins to the ones at the top of the regime. And the consulting, training and participation of Cuban entities in international terrorist activities has allowed the government of the Castro's an income stream that has contributed to making several Castroites into very wealthy money men. Extortion, as a State practice, carried out against businesspeople, politicians and other celebrities has been another strong source of revenue.

Additionally, Communist Cuba has been the supplier of information gathered by its intelligence sources and this has become another route for hard currency to be captured. The enourmous espionage apparatus that has characterized Communist

Cuban despotism has been formulated not only as a mechanism for the survival of the political power but also to traffic in privileged information and to obtain favors from other regimes and terrorist movements. In business, the concessions that are granted to foreign companies usually carry along a system of commissions or gifts that the regime's officials demand and get.

The facts are that Castro Communism has not skimped on producing circumstances so that a few will take advantage and obtain huge sums of money unofficially. Even the exit of Cubans from the national territory is infested with the corruption of officials. The parallel made with this way of doing business with the Mafia is valid. Up to this point we have examined some of the peculiar forms of illicit enrichment utilized by some of Castro's people. The dark and hidden resources of Castro Communism, however, lie not only in the personal coffers of this tightly knit corrupt group. The entire economic machinery of the Castro dictatorship is politically controlled.

Most of the Cuban economy is directly in the hands of the Castro dictatorship. The Revolutionary Armed Forces (FAR) is the institution in charge of handling 70% of the economic sector. The case of Cuban Communism exhibits the characteristics of extreme *nepotism.* The Business Administration Group (GAESA), for example, is a monstrously huge conglomerate emblematic of the mercantilist Castro machine, and at the helm is the son-in-law of the dictator Raúl Castro, Colonel Luis Alberto Rodríguez López-Callejas. Cuban Communism has developed a network of more than 2,500 businesses using the system of autonomous corporations that operate both inside and outside Cuba. Most of them (if not all) doing business abroad operate in secrecy.

The assets of this commercial machinery of the Castro regime, the sly businesses as well as those clearly identified with the official seal, need to be taken away, their structures dismantled and their financial gains placed at the service of the Cuban nation. The amounts collected should be deposited with the Commission for the Recovery of Ill-gotten Funds or an equivalent agency. The same should be done with the personal net worth of the high echelon of the regime and family members who have plundered the nation.

Point 5 Penalize Companies That Are Accomplices and Violators of Labor Laws

Due to reasons of economic survival, Castro Communism had to modify its economy at the beginning of the 1990s. It opened the door for foreign investment in Cuba, establishing arrangements with foreign companies to allow them to participate in the Cuban economy as minority investors, as the Castro regime and related enterprises were to keep a majority interest in this commercial scheme. These business transactions between Communist Cuba and these foreign companies and this hybrid socio-economic system brought about the fixing in place of the most systematic and flagrant violations of labor laws in the world. A version of neo-slavery was thus institutionalized. These companies, which cooperated with Communist despotism by exploiting the Cuban worker, ought to be fined in proportion to the amount they pillaged from the Cuban worker and on account of the degree of complicity they had with the tyranny.

These agreements between the Cuban Communist dictatorship and foreign companies, due to the legal manner in which they were negotiated, granted the role of partners to these businesses. Having a private company with a corporate address in a country where it decides to invest, or to set up operations, seems, at a simple glance, like a normal part of the global reality, but only if and when the laws of the host country are observed. A moral issue arises when the foreign company comes from a free and democratic nation while the country receiving the investment is ruled by a non-democratic regime. Unfortunately, this conflict of principles has suffered the attacks of the counter-culture in its war against democratic ethics. However, in the Cuban case, the problem is not only a question of immoral transactions.

The legality found in the Castro Constitution of 1976 and its laws, decrees and successive public pronouncements has codified the supremacy of the Cuban dictatorial State in the commercial life of the country. This turns the relationship between the foreign company operating in Communist Cuba and the Castro regime, in praxis, into one of complicity. That is, the nature of the relationship itself between a foreign investor company and the Castro government produces, in the exercise of the commercial activity that is regulated by the agreement to operate in Cuba, a series of acts that violate international labor laws and norms. And so, in other words, it goes beyond the dilemma of crossing the line of morality. The issue is not just to invest and to do business with a dictatorship. The most hurtful aspect is to go into business with the Castro regime and to have to comply, mandatorily, with the demands of the rules of the game, which potentially constitute criminal activity.

Castro Communism, and consequently the foreign companies that do business with it, exploit the Cuban worker. The Castro dictatorship expropriates from the Cuban worker between 80% and 92% of his remuneration. A foreign company pays a government agency and this agency redistributes to the worker the remaining 8% or 20%. The Cuban worker cannot be hired directly by the foreign company. The regime is the one that selects the worker and sends him in. We could go on, as it is a long list regarding the kinds of violations that have been committed and are being committed against the workers in Cuba. We will limit the discussion to only four international agreements.

The Protection of Wages Convention (No. 95, Article 9) of 1949 of the International Labor Organization (ILO) prohibits that a worker be deprived of part of his salary. This includes the party that contracted for the labor, even if it is a state agency.

The Right to Organize and Collective Bargaining Convention (No. 98) of 1949 by the ILO makes it illegal to prohibit the right of a worker to organize and to belong to a labor union independent from the government in order to be able to use collective bargaining without governmental interference. The Employment Policy Convention (No. 122) of 1964 by the ILO stipulates that workers are free to choose their employment without discriminatory obstacles. The U.N. Universal Declaration of Human Rights of 1949, it its Article 23, essentially compiles the principles of the aforementioned three conventions.

All enterprises operating in Communist Cuba enjoy minimal autonomy having to bend to any dictum or arbitrariness coming from a dictatorship that operates tyrannically. This reality and the civilized norms that exist at an international level, expressly prohibit what business consortiums are doing with the Castro´s.

This makes any company doing business in Cuba, an accomplice of a crime.

Point 6 Confiscated or Trafficked-in Properties

Castro's Communist project, upon its consolidation of power, launched a wholesale process aimed at abolishing the private property of Cubans. It is estimated that in 1959, when Cuba had a population of just over 6 million people, there were more than 255,000 businesses consisting of factories, business firms and farms and more than 1,800,000 private homes. The draconian pillage that Cuban Communism carried out, not only upset the socio-economic and political order in the country, but also represents the greatest theft of private property in the Western Hemisphere. What should be done in the controversial matter of confiscated property once Cuba is free?

This is one of the prickliest topics in the Cuban drama. On the one hand, if the harm of institutionalized theft is not corrected, which is in effect what the Castro regime has done, this would be a validation of the holdup and would encourage impunity. On the other hand, in the case of homes, it would not be advisable or right to kick people out of their homes or apartments where they have been living for a long time. Is there room to reconcile this dilemma? Yes, solutions can be found and it is necessary to resolve the issue of property expropriated by the Castro´s from people who are, in effect, also victims of Communism as their properties were stolen. First let's talk about the case of expropriated businesses.

Despite the apparent enormity of the claims given the high number of those affected, in practice this doesn't appear to be as large a problem as it is portrayed initially. In the case of small and medium businesses, this is the case. The main reason is the calendar and geography. As many of the former owners have passed away and their families and heirs have remade their lives in another country, it is not probable that they will want to return to take charge of a business which was looted. Large companies, especially all that transferred their corporate structures into exile, have a high probability to want (and they ought to) to retake the reins that the Communists took away. There we also see good news. And not only on account of the justice involved in seeing businesses, many of them family ones, being returned to their legitimate owners, but also for the innovation, know-how and capital that these can bring to bear in order to revitalize the new Cuba.

How then to proceed? If the business or its equivalent is functioning at the hands of the State, it can be transferred directly to the old owners, their families or heirs. In the case of a business asset now in possession of a foreign enterprise, the free Cuban government should initiate legal action to remedy the situation. When the company in question was "sold" or leased by the Castro dictatorship, this makes that transaction null, as it constitutes trafficking in stolen property. Large companies that were confiscated have a greater chance of being available for this type of claim. Although the greatest number of business properties belonged to Cubans, any person or foreign business entity which suffered the spoliation of their properties has the right and access to judicial action to get relief for damages.

In the case of houses that were usurped by Castro Communism this represent a bit more complex situation, though not one incapable of being resolved. When the property in question is being inhabited by someone or by families associated with the dictatorial elite, or if it is part of assets misappropriated, immediately the property needs to be returned to the legitimate owner, family members or heirs. In situations where there are families living in the houses or apartments in question, and if these are not involved criminally with Castro Communism, they shall not be removed from the residence. These families had no part in the theft carried out by the State, and as such need not be penalized. How then can these cases be resolved?

The free and democratic Cuban State needs to open a Commission on Confiscated Properties to compile the names of all the affected. In cases where the property is an occupied home, the owner needs to receive some sort of indemnification, the amount of which at this time is impossible to calculate, as it would depend on a series of factors related to what is taken in and available in a fund established for the purpose of indemnifying the victims. One thing is sure, those victims of crimes against humanity and other gross human rights violations get priority regarding the restitution of confiscated material assets. Ultimately, if this fund were to have insufficient amounts to give restitution to those affected by the theft of their property, and if no other home or business can be found where to relocate them, they would be issued a sum in government bonds or in the stock of corporations recovered, purged, and functioning.

Experience shows us that any attempt to remedy the damages caused by the actions of totalitarian regimes is always insufficient. The action to rescue is good and just, and we need to say no to impunity on the road to correct this huge harm that a system headed up by a group of criminals in charge of a country were able to do. It is not only proper and worthwhile but morally mandatory.

Point 7 Repudiation of Castro-era Debt

Communist Cuba has been, very possibly, the greatest debtor per capita in the world, when we include the total and true debts owed to the former USSR and Venezuela. The Cuban democracy should not, nor does it have to recognize, the debt incurred by the Castro dictatorship. A point of order and for clarification is required to understand the morality behind the proposal made of repudiating the financial obligations that the Castro regime acquired.

Democratic government represents the society that elected them. These reflect the sovereign will of the people and are the political expression of a nation. In democracies, the social contract is valid due to the principle of consent that seals the agreement, although as always keeping in mind that all governments have limits imposed on them by the natural rights of the governed. The notion of holding free and competitive elections, and the guarantee of freedom of expression, information and association, extends to the people a veto power in practice over any action or set of actions they don't want. When something happens that causes a loss of confidence on the part of the people, such as taking away their power of making the decisions about the course the country should take, the sovereign people can decide in the ballot box.

That is why, when there are changes of government, due to alternating administrations by political parties, for example, the society and the new government assumes as their own, the consequences of the actions of the previous government. This includes the public debts acquired. This is part of the social contract in a democratic regime. When we talk of a dictatorship, everything changes. The difference gets worse when we talk about a regime of total domination, as the one that still holds sway in Cuba today.

Dictatorial regimes, such as Castro's, govern without the consent of the governed. The totalitarian particulars of it extend its command to a much wider and deep reach over the country and its citizens. The leadership characteristics of it are: sultanistic, nepotistic and dynastic, which in the Cuban context add a potent dosage of arbitrariness and capricious governance. Cuban society, however, has not had the opportunity ever to determine if it accepted or not the social contract of Castro Communism. This arrangement between the government and the governed was imposed through deceit and after its imposition it has been reinforced by terror and repression. And so in Cuba there is no legitimate social contract with popular consent.

The principle that supports the previous explanations seeks to establish the differentiation that exists between debts acquired by a democratic government and those by a totalitarian dictatorship, and the different obligations that correspond to the populations in each of these cases. In the former case (democracy) the debt passes on to the people, due to the nature of the relationship between the government and the governed, and the rules of free elections and alternatives available in the democratic socio-political scheme. Debts obtained by totalitarian regimes, as is the case of Castro Communism; do not transfer over to the people due to the inexistent connection of consensual legitimacy.

The Castro dictatorship launched, as soon as it got in power, a war to promote the Communist revolution with its vision of class struggle throughout the globe. Not everything was warlike or due to an ideology or a system. Castro Communism once in power turned several Cubans into millionaires, all behind the back of international law. At the same time, it plunged a whole nation into an abysmal poverty and the rest was forced to have to abandon the country. For all these reasons, the debt negotiated by the Castro government should die and be buried with the regime. Any institution or lender State which tries to access the courts to try to force a free Cuba to pay the debts of the Castro´s and their dictatorship needs to find a democratic free State ready and energized to counter-sue since the lender was in collusion with the tyrannical regime, whose record and pattern in committing crimes against humanity and as a gross violator of human rights is well-known.

Point 8 The Constitution

The Constitution of 1976, as amended in 1992 and 2002, its laws, and its penal code should be voided and annulled immediately in a free and democratic Cuba. The Castro legality has been an instrument, inherently, for the rationalization and reinforcement of tyrannical power. They violate, intrinsically, the natural rights of Cubans. Constitutional articles number 39, 53, 62, 72 and the preemptive "pre-criminal" laws of the Penal Code against "potentially dangerous behavior" and "antisocial" conduct (Articles 72, 73.1, 75.1, 82), against "disrespecting laws" (Article 144.1), "disobedience of the State" (Article 147) as well as of cooperation with the U.S. embargo (Article 91), sharply violate fundamental human rights that have no statutes of limitation. The Cuban democracy is incompatible with any adulterated version of the Castro Constitution or of its legality.

Cuba, after being under totalitarian domination for more than 57 years is in no condition to hold a constitutional convention immediately. The reason is clear. Despite the fact that the process of decommunization in general, and of lustration in particular, safeguard against the return of Castro

Communism in the political stage, the fact remains that the counter-culture imposed by the long stay of the Marxist-Leninist dictatorship with personalistic overtones, didn't foster a democratic culture in the population. Consequently, we would run the risk --if a constitutional convention were to be called immediately after the fall of the Castro regime-- that those connected with the former regime, although not tainted with criminal activity per se, would be in a more advantageous position and would probably dominate the process. As a civil society is practically inexistent, Cuba would be left vulnerable to manipulation by sectors friendly to electoral despotism, one of the new innovations to achieve dictatorial control. The Cuban democracy must not take such a chance.

The more sensible step, in line with our history, is to bring back the last democratic magna carta of Cuba, the 1940 Constitution. Some critics point out its potential inapplicability in the present day, arguing that it is too prescriptive, detailed and voluminous with its 286 articles. Alberto Luzárraga, a Cuban exile lawyer and researcher, has conducted numerous projects related to bringing the 1940 Constitution up to date. In effect, his work proposes to amend the last legitimate constitution of republican and sovereign Cuba, modifying a bit more than 100 of its articles. The 1940 Constitution is a great document which, with these modifications, becomes apt for our modern times.

If it were the will of most Cubans to call for a constitutional convention in the new Cuba, I would recommend a waiting period of at least five years after the reinstallation of the 1940 Constitution (and the annulment of the 1976 one). This would provide a conformable time for the strengthening of Cuban society, as well as of the new democratic institutions.

Among the constitutional modifications that should be considered is the issue of dual citizenship for Cubans who live abroad and their children. The tragic episode of the Cuban drama has witnessed more than 20% of its population leave for exile. The Cuban nation is an interesting case of transnational phenomena. The 2 million Cubans that reside outside of the national territory, measured as a productive economic unit, produce a Gross Domestic Product (GDP) many times higher than the 11 million living on the Island.

Exiled Cubans have lived in open societies, in democracies and have for the most part transplanted and rescued genuine Cuban customs, traditions, its history and values. Castro Communism has been able to, with regrettable success, control and distort the history and the other mentioned factors by way of the political control it exercises on the Island. However, that has not been able to be achieved with the Cuban nation that has lived without a State or a national territory of its own, but free and in exile. This is why it is pressing that the Cuban nation, inside and outside of its geographical physical limits, have dual citizenship and representation in a free Cuban government.

Lastly, another important issue that a democratic Cuban government should take up and make it State policy, although this is not necessarily a matter which involves the constitution, is the issue of the Guantanamo Bay Naval Base. Upon the consolidation of democracy in Cuba and the burial of the communist dictatorship, negotiations should begin with the American government so that the United States the territory to the Republic of Cuba. It would be time.

Point 9 Economy

At this point in time, there is in Cuba an economic system of the *socialist mercantilist* variety. It is a hybrid model that features selective and politicized tolerance towards private property, the means of production, market mechanisms, employment hiring, setting of prices and direct foreign investment. The economy is still being commanded from the highest echelons of political power. The level of planning and organization is not centralized, as was the case in this system prior to 1992: the socialist economic model. After that year the Castro regime modified its constitution and has successively continued to redefine the terms of this variety of mercantilism: in 1995 (Law Number 77), in 2004 (Agreement 5290/04), in 2011 (Guidelines), and in 2013 (Law-Decree Number 313). Some prefer to call economic models such as the one in place in Cuba *State capitalism* or *crony capitalism*. What it is definitely not, is a genuine free market system, and much less one guaranteed by the Rule of Law.

It's irrelevant to try to be exact in classifying the operating system used by the Castro's, what is important and what is undeniable is that it doesn't serve to meet the needs of the people of Cuba revealing a series of deficiencies which are prejudicial to that new free Cuban nation having aspirations of total democratization. An economy in the hands of a military oligarchy produces enormous concentrations of wealth in a very small portion of the population as the omnipresent dominion of the economy by the dictatorial State doesn't allow a civil society to produce and prosper. We see how the political power monopolizes the economic sector as well as the non-State and non-foreign sector it tolerates, turning it into courtesans that do not manifest nor exert any legitimate entrepreneurial function, serving only as counterweights for the power of the ruler. It should be clear that with the fall of Castro Communism its inoperative and terribly unfair economic system has to go. Towards which model then should the country go?

Cuba needs an economic model that produces wealth, which extends fairness, which encourages social equilibrium and one that is complementary to democracy as a political system. It needs to be a model of economic organization resting on private property and individual initiative in production. Property rights need to receive strong legal protection. In this regard, as in many other guarantees, the 1940 Constitution was very clear and powerful. The means of production should be in private hands as much as possible, as the overwhelming evidence points to the superiority in productive output of the private sector over the public sector. Private property, additionally, is very important as a guardian *par excellence* of liberty as it establishes a barrier against an extreme or dangerous reach by the State.

Prices and salaries ought to be free of controls right away in order to invigorate Cuba's productive capabilities. Price and salary controls disturb the rational process of setting the true monetary value of goods and services and only serves, in the medium- and long-term, to destroy the productive engine of any society. Empirical evidence shows that in the cases of former socialist-bloc countries in Eastern Europe, that the places where democratization turned out to be most successful were in those where liberalization reforms extended into a deeper layer and with greatest speed. The liberalization of price and salary controls as well as specific quotas is fundamental. These are artificial mechanisms which distorts the economic Law of Supply and Demand.

The *market,* understood as a means and process whereby producers and consumers exchange goods and services, doesn't always work at perfect equilibrium. This is due to, among other factors, but principal among them, the inability of all the actors (producers and consumers) to compete on an even playing field. An authentic and dynamic competition is essential to ensure that the market is operating in the most optimal way. The market fails, gets distorted or becomes irrational when monopolies or cartels interfere in the process. This takes place, typically, when the monopoly can count on the support of the State. The monopolization of economic activities brings with it, even worse problems in the political realm for this reason. In dictatorships it is predictable and characteristic of powerful corporations to seek benefits from political power and protection from their competitors. In democratic regimes, favoritism on the part of a government towards a few businesses helps takes away the competitive edge of others and undermines the purpose of self-governance, corrupting the social balance that is so fundamental in a democracy.

And so, the economic model for a free Cuba should include solid legal and structural mechanisms to inherently fight against the formation of monopolies and of its byproduct in society, oligarchies. No State need be coopted by business interests or private groups. The democratic ethic urges us to host, in the economic realm, a system that stops any tendency towards monopolization or of absorption by the State for private purposes.

Poverty need not be a permanent phase in the life of any Cuban, as has been the case in this long night of Castro Communism. The economic model that a democratic Cuba should adopt should include systemic devices to ease *social mobility*. This requires, in the realm of the labor market, flexible labor laws that do not incentivize a static labor sector. When an employer is burdened above his ability to comply and to also make a profit, he stops employing people or has to close his doors. A greater elasticity in labor laws provides workers with greater opportunities to look for the employer or contractor that offers them the best options for their talents. Naturally, all labor hiring needs to be direct and free. Through labor union a worker may also accede to the labor market, if he so prefers.

This is another alternative that may be attractive, both for a company (it would be assured of hiring qualified personnel) as well as for the worker (the trade union serves as a filter).

In order to develop a more conducive climate for a dynamic labor market, businesses (small, medium and large) should be freed from having to pay for welfare benefits for their employees. This responsibility should fall on the State. The idea is that lesser the obstacles for a domestic or foreign company to open and keep operations in Cuba, the lesser the cost of adding a Cuban worker would be. The idea is simple, if Cubans have more options in seeking jobs, they will thus have better remuneration and more work alternatives and nobody would have to remain at a job only on account of the fringe benefits, such as health insurance.

Transparency and access to information are crucial for an open and free society to be informed about available job opportunities. Consequently, the State of a new Cuba should take on a proactive role in facilitating a match between a worker looking for work and an enterprise that is looking for one. The government needs to have at its disposal a great deal of information about job openings and the curriculum vitae of job seekers, in an accessible and updated way. Therefore a digital database needs to be built which would be free, of easy access and easy to understand and use in order to let the population know about available job offerings while informing employers by providing information about the Cuban labor market. The goal being for employees and employers, mutually, to have access to a mechanism that promotes a vibrant economy, offers an attractive employment climate and a country worthy of anyone who wishes to work and to get ahead.

A socio-economic model that is pro-growth and emphasizes mobility, justice and social equilibrium, at the same time, can only be achieved if there is in place a public services and welfare network including an extensive, modern and first-class social security system. We will mention a part of the social security program that a free and democratic Cuba should have. To begin with, it is indispensable to have a health system that is not only accessible for all but also of high quality. Cuban health needs to combine private and public medicine. They can coexist perfectly well, offering more options to Cubans than otherwise. The system of public medical coverage would include a network of community health centers, clinics and hospitals, all of them offering universal medical care available to the whole of the population. The private system would mimic the private medicine that existed before Communism offered by mutualist associations, with private doctor's offices and with a scheme of health maintenance organizations that the Cuban exiles transported and built upon in the U.S. after leaving the island.

Education in a democratic Cuba should also include both a public and a private option. The public school system should be universal, offering education from kindergarten to postgraduate level. Private education should coexist and school vouchers could also be made available whereby monies from public schools could be transferred to a private school, without any additional cost to the parents. Public education cannot be limited only to basic and academic learning but it should also extend to vocational education including trade schools. This would give to Cubans a wide variety of educational opportunities.

The social security network should include, additionally, unemployment coverage and welfare assistance, job and vocational retraining, public access to cultural resources such as museums, libraries, parks, art, literature and cinema centers, etc, assistance for people with disabilities or senior citizens, public legal assistance, access to a public defender, and other considerations or an urgent and vital importance. We do not mean to say that we need to establish a social welfare State, but rather we need to develop an equitable socio-economic system, transparent, with social harmony and in an environment where the working class and the business class do not have to carry the burden of obtaining, paying and providing certain basic goods and services such as those mentioned above. What existing socio-economic model is perhaps close to all this?

Understanding that each country is a *sui generis* phenomenon, and that when applying political and economic schemes local peculiarities are attached by each nation which now subscribes to them, the model of the *market social economy* ("the German model") or as it is known in the social sciences, *ordoliberalism*, would be a fairly close system in a practical sense to the one being recommended for a free Cuba in a democracy. "Ordo" stands for Latin "order".

This economic model and school of thought is an offshoot of classic liberalism under the notion that an unattended market, one lacking the checks and balances of an arbiter, can be manipulated by business interests or by the political class which in collusion could make a healthy and true competition impossible.

Other versions supported in theory by the same name of free enterprise, raise flags and so care needs to be taken as not to become perverted: *popular capitalism* and *competitive capitalism*. The premise behind all these schools of thought includes the proposition that commercial interests seek and wish, by nature, the elimination of competition. These commercial interests look for support from politicians to advance those purposes in order to avoid having to face competitors. The formation of cartels by economic blocs, companies that dominate markets or by monopolies is evidence of prejudicial distortion to the principle of competition which is a key factor for a market to fulfill its function of producing the best goods and services with a fair base of participation. Other components of a healthy economy include being able to avoid storms upon the economic state of a country, especially to prevent the damage that is typically self-inflicted by the erroneous management of politicians.

The greatest economic evil is inflation. It slams the hardest those that have the least. That is why it is basic for the Cuban free government to adopt policies that avoid the mistakes of programs that ease inflationary explosions. There are two branches of economic policy that impact the inflation caused, potentially, by erroneous formulas. A democratic Cuba should avoid falling into schemes that stimulate galloping inflation. These two areas of economic policy are: *monetary policy* and *fiscal policy.*

The free Cuban state, in conjunction with economists and politicians, should follow a monetary policy of stability and predictability in their approach regarding the money supply and its circulation. The currency in circulation should be only one, the Cuban peso. Price stability and predictability in the circulation of pesos is important to have an economy of positive growth and low inflation under control. Another aspect of monetary policy is the rate of interest set by the Central Bank to stimulate the economy at times of slow growth or negative growth or in order to put the brakes on the economy to avoid an increased price level (inflation).

There are mechanisms to avoid the politicizing of economic tools which, if left to unbridled ideological impulses or special interests, could accelerate or decelerate the economy, which are subject to manipulation. Therefore, it would be prudent to have in place a permanent framework of policies that are aimed to work on "automatic pilot". In this fashion, changes in administrations or laws would not alter stability and predictability, two irreplaceable factors in the ordering of a successful economy.

Taylor's Law, named after economist John B. Taylor, codifies norms and parameters regarding how the Central Bank needs to proceed in increasing or lowering interest rates in the management of monetary policy. It offers specific and pre-established guidelines that aim to provide a signal as to when it needs to act to increase or decrease interest rates. The factors to look for are: the percentage rate of inflation; The Gross Domestic Product (GDP); the current rate of interest. What is good about these formularies is that they take away politics from economic measures offering more guarantees that the Central Bank will follow coherent and rational economic postures.

Regarding fiscal policy in a free and democratic Cuba, a course of transparency should be set including low expenses and taxes and one not very complicated. Corruption is a major problem in any society. The most effective formula to minimize it is to have a system of absolute transparency in all public expenditures, in all bids, in all political sessions, in all business with the State, in all government finances with all public officials, and that all this information should be digitized and easy to access. The 1940 Constitution contains strong mechanisms to keep in line corruption and fraud.

Public expenditures should remain paired with the revenues of the State. There are also attractive options to contain unbridled fiscal deficits. These policies aim to establish ceilings on public expenditures placing them on "automatic pilot" in such a way depoliticizing a bit the process of spending other people's money. These formulas establish limits regarding what can be spent, in accordance with various factors that include GDP, the rate of economic growth, the unemployment rate and the revenues entering the coffers of the government. Having a pre-set limit on public spending tied to the aforementioned factors (GDP, rates of economic growth, unemployment, amount of revenue) helps to avoid the fiscal disarrays that characterize debtor countries, some of them even going into bankruptcy.

As can be seen, in order to able to offer the best goods and services, to have a high standard of living with fairness and opportunity for upward mobility, it is indispensable that Cuba obtain appreciably high levels of economic growth. And to do this and to pay for the social security program we advocate, there has to be an economic climate favorable for robust economic activity. For this purpose the rate of taxation should be as low as possible, so as not to discourage an individual's productivity or that of an enterprise, and one that does not stimulate unbridled consumerism.

Taking into account all the policy tools available to a State to generate revenue to be spent in public goods and services by means of taxation, an option that Cubans should consider is the *Value Added Tax* (VAT) as a substitute for the income tax for individuals and families. This method is simpler, it stimulates productivity as it does not penalize earning money and it helps to forge a more solid economy, as it is less dependent on cycles or spurts in consumption. Companies would pay taxes on their profits of between 5% and 10%. This would make Cuba an attractive place to invest.

In this globalized world, Cuba has the exquisite opportunity to become, in a free and open society, an economic giant. Free trade with other nations or blocs of countries is something to strive for. Of course, always after giving priority to national interests, domestic industries and social costs looked at comprehensively, with a long term focus, when looking at the benefits a trade pact might afford. Free commercial interactions, yet just and beneficial for all Cubans, should be the principle standard to guide international trade policy.

Point 10 System of Government

The semi-presidential model propitiated by the 1940 Constitution or the presidential type supported by the 1901 Constitution, offer adequate systems of government for a functional democracy. Both systems of democratic governance contain the necessary mechanisms to avoid the predominance of one branch over another (executive, legislative and judicial) or to an unbalance and potential abuses of power. These indispensable elements of a democracy are: *separation of powers*, *control of constitutionality* and other *checks and balances.* There are additional aspects that should be included or amended in the Cuban case in order to avoid the potential problems of corruption and the interference of special interests in the political process. One of them would be the *public financing* of political campaigns.

The problem of allowing private monies in electoral contests is the ostentatious possibility of corrupting the political process for various reasons. The lack of funds deprives those that lack funding from competing in equal terms, allowing the materialization of laws and exemptions to them in obedience to special interests, handing an oversized influence to persons who are not elected by the sovereign people. For these and other reasons, the financing of elections strictly by means of public funds would be the best option to combat toxic deficiencies to good governance.

The funds earmarked for elections should be dispersed directly to the candidates in primary elections rather than to political parties. This would avoid favoritism among party operatives within the process of selecting candidates, and would provide the best possibility for attracting new people into the process. Once one candidate has captured the nomination of his or her party for the seat in play, in the following general elections public funds ought to be distributed half for the party and the other half for the individual candidate. For a party to qualify to obtain public funds it would have to gather a minimum of a third of the possible votes.